This book belongs to

Jessica Oakley
Easter 1995

All-time Favorite Bible Stories of the New Testament

V. Gilbert Beers
Ronald A. Beers

Illustrated by
Daniel J. Hochstatter

Thomas Nelson Publishers, Inc.   Nashville, Tennessee

Copyright © 1991 by Educational Publishing Concepts, Inc., Wheaton, IL
Exclusive Distribution by Thomas Nelson Publishers, Inc., Nashville, TN

A Word to Parents

Some Bible stories deserve to be called "All-time Favorites."

That's because they are. These were your favorite Bible stories when you were a child. Perhaps they were your parents' favorite Bible stories when they were children, too. Now they can become favorites for your children.

Why are some stories favorites? These are the stories with unforgettable characters, dramatic events, and wonderful objects. Such as the humble yet miraculous birth of Jesus; and the exciting way God protected Him from the evil King Herod. Children will enjoy reading about the child Jesus, too, and that He had parents to obey just as they do.

The plan of God becomes clear as Jesus grows and His ministry develops. He enters Jerusalem, cleans the temple and continues teaching about His Father.

The story of Jesus' betrayal and death will touch your child's heart, while the account of His resurrection may bring opportunity for him to believe and ask Jesus into his heart.

It's thrilling to read how evil Saul was converted and began preaching about the very God he once persecuted. You'll read how Jesus' followers trusted God through difficult times as they constantly shared the Good News.

The New Testament is filled with stories of great Christians who were just ordinary people. Share these stories with your children and watch these all-time favorite stories become their all-time favorites, too.

—*V. Gilbert & Ronald A. Beers*

All-time Favorite Bible Stories of the New Testament

V. Gilbert Beers, Ronald A. Beers

Contents

Jesus' Birth Announced

Mary was confused and frightened when she saw the Angel Gabriel appear before her. "Good news for you, young lady," the angel said to her. "God is with you."

Of course Mary was not sure what to say. So she listened as the angel kept on speaking.

"Don't be afraid, Mary. God has something special for you. You will have a baby boy and will name Him Jesus. He will be a great person, the Son of God. He will be a king forever."

"But I have never been married," Mary argued. "How can I have a baby?" Mary was engaged to Joseph, one of King David's descendants. But they had not lived together yet.

"The Holy Spirit will come to you, and God's power will be upon you," the angel answered. "This baby will be God's Son. God will be His Father." Then the angel told Mary about her cousin Elizabeth. "Six months ago Elizabeth found that she would have a baby," the angel said. "Every promise God makes will come true."

"I am God's servant," Mary said. "I will do whatever He wants. Let everything you said happen."

Then the angel was gone.

Jesus Is Born

The Roman Emperor Caesar Augustus, ruled over much of the world at the time of these stories. He decided to take a census of all the people of his empire, so he gave his people orders to do this. By the way, that was about the same time when Quirinius was governor of Syria.

The census required everyone to go back to the place where their ancestors had lived. There people would register by families. Joseph was a member of the family that had come from King David. So he had to go to Bethlehem in Judea, where King David had lived as a boy.

So Joseph took Mary, who was almost ready to have her child, and made his way to Bethlehem. But when they arrived there was no room in the inn, so they had to stay in the stable with animals. That night, Mary's baby was born. She wrapped Him in long strips of cloth, and laid Him in a manger, where the animals ate.

Eight days later, at the circumcision ceremony, this boy would be named Jesus. That was what the angel had told Mary that God wanted. Of course Mary wanted to obey God.

Angels Appear to the Shepherds

One wonderful night, Jesus was born in Bethlehem. Not far away, in some fields outside town, shepherds watched their flocks of sheep. Suddenly an angel appeared to the shepherds. A bright light shined upon them. It was a special light from God. Of course the shepherds were surprised and frightened. But the angel tried to comfort them.

"Don't be afraid," the angel said. "I have wonderful news. It is the most wonderful news that anyone has ever heard. But this news is for all people everywhere. The Savior, God's Son, has been born tonight in Bethlehem. You may see Him there, wrapped in strips of cloth, lying in a manger."

A great choir of angels appeared in the night sky, and began praising God. "Glory to God!" the great angel choir sang. "Glory to God in the highest. Peace to all who please Him here on earth."

The shepherds had never heard such a wonderful choir. They had never heard such a wonderful song. What a night that was on the hills outside Bethlehem!

Shepherds Worship Jesus

When the great choir of angels was through singing, it suddenly disappeared. The shepherds could not see the angels now, for they had gone back to heaven. That's where the angels had been before they appeared to the shepherds.

The night sky was empty again except for the stars. The hills were quiet again except for a quiet "baa" from a sheep here and there.

The shepherds stared at each other for a while. Had they really seen the angels? Had they really heard the choir singing? Had they heard the angel tell about the Savior, God's Son? Suddenly the shepherds knew what a wonderful thing they had heard. The Savior was born tonight, in Bethlehem!

"Let's go now to see Him!" the shepherds said to one another. "Let's see this Baby the Lord has told us about." The shepherds hurried to Bethlehem and found the stable where Mary and Joseph were staying.

How excited they were to see Baby Jesus, lying in the manger. This news was too good to keep. The shepherds went everywhere, telling the good news about the Savior who was born. People listened carefully, for this was good news that everyone had waited to hear.

Mary didn't say much about these things. But she was so happy and her heart was filled, like a chest full of treasure. Many times after that she thought about this wonderful night.

At last the shepherds went back to their sheep. They praised God often for the angels who had come to see them. And they praised God that they could see the Savior, the Baby Jesus.

Simeon and Anna Honor Jesus

When Jesus was eight days old, His parents circumcised Him, just as all good Hebrew parents did on the eighth day. There was a party, or ceremony, and Jesus was named on that day also. Mary and Joseph named Him Jesus, as the angel had told Mary long before He was born.

Some time after that, Mary and Joseph went to the temple, God's house, for another ceremony. Like other Hebrew mothers, Mary would be purified on that day, following the birth of her child. She would give an offering of two turtledoves or two pigeons, for that was what the law said she should do. Since Jesus was Mary's first son, she must also give Him to God.

While Mary and Joseph were there in God's house, an old man named Simeon saw them. The Holy Spirit had shown him that he would not die until he had seen the Savior. When he saw Jesus, he knew this Baby was the Savior he had waited to see. Simeon took Baby Jesus into his arms and praised God.

Mary and Joseph listened to all this and wondered. What did all this mean?

Simeon spoke to Mary next. "Some day you will be deeply hurt, for this Boy will be rejected by many of His own people. But He will also bring great joy to many others."

While Simeon was still talking, an old woman named Anna came along. She was a woman of God who lived there in the temple. When Anna saw Jesus, she began thanking God for Him. She knew that this was God's Son, the Savior. She began telling others that the Savior had come at last.

Mary and Joseph knew for certain now that this Boy was God's Son, the Savior. They must have thanked God many times that He had come at last.

Wise Men See a Star

When Jesus was born in Bethlehem, some wise men lived in a faraway land to the east. One night they saw a bright star they had never seen before. They knew this star was special, for it told them that a great King had been born.

The wise men set out at once to find this new King. They followed the star until it led them to the land of Israel. The wise men began asking people in Jerusalem about this new King. "Where is the new King of the Jews?" they asked. "We have seen His star in the east. We have come to worship Him."

King Herod was disturbed when he heard what these men were asking. He was the king. He did not want any other king to come and take his kingdom from him. People began whispering things about this King all over Jerusalem. So Herod called for the Jewish religious leaders.

"Do the prophets tell where this King will be born?" he asked.

"Yes, they do," the leaders answered. "The Prophet Micah wrote that a new Ruler would be born in Bethlehem."

When Herod heard that, he sent a message for the wise men to come to see him. "When did you first see the star?" he asked them. When they told him, Herod said, "Go and search for the Child in Bethlehem. When you find Him, come back here and let me know. Then I may go and worship Him, too."

Herod actually was plotting to kill this new King. He would not let another king take his kingdom from him.

The wise men did not know about Herod's plans. They were happy now that they had learned where this new King had been born. They would leave for Bethlehem immediately to find the new King.

Wise Men Visit Jesus

When the wise men left King Herod, they headed toward Bethlehem. There they would find the great King, the Savior. That's what the Jewish religious leaders had read in Micah, the Prophet.

On the way the special star they had seen appeared to them again. It led them to Bethlehem and stood over the house where Jesus lived with Mary and Joseph. When the wise men went into the house, they saw little Jesus at last. Then they knelt down before Him and worshiped Him.

These men had brought special gifts with them, which they gave to little Jesus now. There was gold, frankincense and myrrh. Gold was used for money at that time. Frankincense and myrrh were expensive spices. Sometimes they were used in God's house when people worshiped Him there. That was a wonderful day for these wise men. They must have had a hundred questions to ask Mary and Joseph.

That night God warned the wise men in a dream. They must not go back to King Herod. They must go home some other way, because Herod wanted to kill young Jesus. The wise men did what God told them. They went home without telling Herod what they had learned.

Mary and Joseph thought often about this visit from the wise men. They knew by this time that Jesus was God's Son, the Savior and great King. But they had never expected a visit like this!

The Flight to Egypt

When the wise men were gone, Mary and Joseph looked again at the wonderful gifts the wise men had brought. There was gold, and frankincense and myrrh. They had never seen such beautiful gifts before.

That night an angel visited Joseph in a dream. "Get up!" the angel urged. "You must leave now for Egypt. Take Jesus and Mary and go! Hurry! King Herod plans to kill Jesus, so you must stay in Egypt until I tell you to leave." Joseph got up immediately. That same night he left for Egypt with Mary and Jesus. There they stayed until they heard again from the angel.

Before long, King Herod realized that the wise men were not coming back to see him. He was angry for he had made plans to kill little Jesus. But how could he kill Jesus when he did not know which child He was?

Herod knew only that Jesus was a boy somewhere in Bethlehem and that He was under two years old. "Kill them all!" Herod screamed. "Kill every boy in Bethlehem under two years old! Kill every boy around Bethlehem, too!" The wise men had told Herod that they had seen the star almost two years ago. That's why Herod killed all the boys two years and younger.

Many years before, the Prophet Jeremiah said this would happen. "There will be screams and crying around this region," he wrote. "Women will cry for their children and nobody can comfort them, for their children will be dead."

The mothers of Bethlehem did cry and scream for their dead boys. Wicked King Herod made many families hurt and cry. But he did not kill little Jesus. God's angel had taken care of Him and kept Him safe.

The Return to Nazareth

Mary and Joseph must have wondered each day how long they would have to stay in Egypt. An angel of God had told Joseph to take Mary and Jesus there. The angel had said they must stay in Egypt until he told them to leave. So the days and months passed.

Then one night an angel appeared to Joseph again in a dream. "Get up and take Jesus and His mother back to Israel," the angel said. "King Herod is dead."

Joseph left with Mary and Jesus. But on the way, he heard that Herod's son, Archelaus, was the new king. Would he be as bad as his father? Would he also want to kill little Jesus? What should he do? That night, an angel of God told Joseph not to go back to Bethlehem. So Joseph took Mary and Jesus to Nazareth, in Galilee, instead. This was the town where Joseph and Mary had lived before Jesus was born. Some prophets had written about this many years before. They said that Jesus would be called a Nazarene, a man who lived at Nazareth.

Mary and Joseph were home at last. What a lot of things had happened since they left! But now they could raise the boy Jesus in their home town. Now they could see Him grow up where they had lived so many years.

Jesus and the Carpenter's Shop

At last Mary and Joseph were home in Nazareth. This had been their home town before Jesus was born. But they had left to go to Bethlehem to visit. The Roman emperor, who ruled the land, said they had to put their names on a census list there. And while they were there, Jesus was born. But they couldn't even stay at Bethlehem. An angel told them to take Jesus to Egypt. There they lived until the angel said they could come home.

Now that they were home, Joseph set up his carpenter's shop again. Each boy in Israel learned to do some special kind of work, usually from their father. Carpentry was the work that Joseph had learned when he grew up. That was the work he did as a man. Now Joseph would teach Jesus how to be a carpenter. The boy Jesus made many things from wood. He hammered and sawed. He cut and polished. He made chairs and tables. He made bowls and wagon wheels. Joseph was glad that he could teach the boy Jesus to be a carpenter. And Jesus was glad that He could work with wood, just as Joseph did.

Jesus and the Teachers

Each year the boy Jesus went to Jerusalem with His family for the great Passover feast. It was like a big party, with everyone in the country invited. When Jesus was twelve, He went with His family again to the Passover. As usual, they ate and talked with friends and relatives.

When at last the feast was over, crowds of people gathered in caravans and headed back to their homes. Jesus' family headed back toward Nazareth. There were aunts and uncles and cousins and many other family members in this caravan. It wasn't unusual for a boy to be walking with an uncle or aunt or cousin. So it wasn't until that evening, when the caravan stopped for the night to rest, that Mary and Joseph realized that Jesus was not there. They looked everywhere, with every aunt and uncle and cousin they could find. But Jesus was not with them.

At last they headed back to Jerusalem. Mary and Joseph looked everywhere they could to find Jesus. At last, three days later, they found Him. There He was, sitting in the temple, God's house, talking with the teachers. Jesus was asking some very tough questions and giving some very good answers.

"Why have You done this to us?" Mary asked the boy Jesus. "Your father and I have been worried. We have looked for You everywhere."

"Didn't you know I would be in My Father's house?" Jesus asked. Jesus went back home to Nazareth with Joseph and Mary. He was an obedient boy, as you would expect.

Mary thought often about what had happened. She must have wondered what it all meant. So Jesus grew up there in Nazareth. He became a tall, wise, young Man. God loved Him, and so did those who knew Him.

Jesus' Triumphal Entry into Jerusalem

Jesus and His friends were near Bethany and Bethphage on the Mount of Olives. It was time for Him to go into Jerusalem. Now He would ride in on a donkey. That was the way kings went into a city in those days. In this way, Jesus would show people He was God's Son.

"Go into this village and you will find a colt tied," Jesus told some friends. "Bring it to Me. If anyone asks, tell him I need it."

The men found the colt. Some people asked what they were doing. They told them Jesus needed it. Then they brought the colt to Jesus. They put clothes on the colt's back and Jesus sat on it.

As Jesus rode toward Jerusalem, people ran out to meet Him. They cut branches and put them on the road where Jesus would ride. Some even put their clothes on the road.

"Praise God!" people shouted. "Praise King David's descendant! Praise the one who comes in the name of the Lord."

Of course this stirred excitement in Jerusalem. Some religious leaders were angry. "Tell these people to stop saying such things," they told Jesus. "If I do, these stones will cry out," Jesus answered.

Jesus rode on the donkey's colt into Jerusalem. Many years before, the prophet Zechariah had said this would happen. "Your king is coming, humble and riding on a donkey," he said. That was the way kings rode into a city in those days. Jesus was greater than a king. He was God's Son.

Jesus at the Temple

When Jesus rode into Jerusalem He went to the temple. People were buying and selling things in the courtyard there. Money changers were trading their money for foreign money. People needed the money changers' money to buy things in the temple. But these money changers cheated people. They charged more for their money than it was worth.

Others were selling doves. These were used in offerings to the Lord.

Jesus began to throw out the people who were selling. He turned over the money changers' tables. Their money spilled on the ground.

"My house is a house of prayer," Jesus said. "That is what the Bible says. But you have made it a house of thieves."

The temple leaders saw what Jesus did. They were angry. They wanted to kill Jesus.

Each day Jesus came to the temple. He taught the people about God. The people listened. They wanted to know what Jesus was saying.

The temple leaders could not hurt Jesus now. The people would not let them. They would have to wait.

Each night Jesus left Jerusalem and went back to Bethany. He would be safe there with friends.

Jesus Teaches with Stories

"Who said You could do what You do?" some leaders asked Jesus one day. "Who said You could teach what You do?"

Jesus knew it was a trap. These people wanted Jesus to say something wrong. If He did, they would be able to kill Him.

What if Jesus said that God told Him to do these things? The leaders would say He claimed to be from God. That was called blasphemy. They could kill Him for that. What if He said someone else told Him to do these things? That wasn't good enough. Only God could tell someone what to do at the temple. No answer would be good enough. What should Jesus do?

"I will answer your question if you answer Mine," Jesus said. "Who told John the Baptist what to do?"

Now the leaders were trapped. If they said "God did," Jesus would ask why they didn't listen to John. If they said "someone else did," the people would be angry. The people thought God told John what to do.

"We don't know," said the leaders.

"Then I will not tell you who said I could do these things," Jesus answered.

Jesus began to teach the people with stories. These stories are called parables. They have two meanings. One is what the story says. The other is what the story tells about God and heaven.

Jesus could teach many things through these stories. Some people wanted to learn from Jesus. They would know what these stories meant. Others wanted to hurt Jesus. They would not know what the stories meant.

Judas Takes Thirty Pieces of Silver

Judas Iscariot was one of Jesus' twelve special helpers. But he was not a good man. He even let Satan tell him what to do. Judas had been with Jesus for a long time. He had heard Jesus teach and watched His miracles. But he did not truly love Jesus. He loved money more than Jesus.

That is why Judas went to see the chief priests and officers of the temple guard. These people wanted to kill Jesus. Now Judas would help them.

"What will you pay me to betray Jesus?" Judas asked. He was offering to help them capture his friend. He would sell his friend to these men for money.

"Thirty pieces of silver," the men answered. So they counted thirty silver coins and gave them to Judas. They were glad to pay Judas this money. They would pay lots of money to capture Jesus and kill Him. These men were jealous of the things Jesus did. They wanted people to follow them instead of following Jesus.

Judas took the money. He would betray Jesus for thirty silver coins. When he left, he began to look for a time and place to betray Jesus. He knew he would have to do this quietly. He must not let the people know what he was doing. If they found out they would stop him.

Preparing for the Last Supper

The time had come for the Passover. This was also called the Festival of Unleavened Bread. Today was the day when the lambs were killed for the Passover supper. Jesus asked Peter and John to get their Passover supper ready. This supper would be their last supper together. We remember it today when we have communion. Sometimes we call the supper they ate together The Last Supper.

"Will you do this for us?" Jesus asked them.

"Where should we eat?" they asked.

"When you go into Jerusalem, you will meet a man with a jar of water," Jesus said.

"Follow him to the house where he is going. Ask the owner about our room. He will show you a large upstairs room. You will get that room ready for our supper."

Peter and John went into Jerusalem. Everything happened the way Jesus said it would. They met a man with a jar of water. They followed the man to a house and asked the owner about a room. The owner showed them the room where they would eat the supper together.

Peter and John got the Passover supper ready. Now Jesus and His friends could eat it together. Now they would have a pleasant room for The Last Supper.

The Last Supper

Peter and John had prepared the food for the Passover supper. Now it was evening and Jesus had come. His twelve special helpers were there too. It was time to eat the supper in the upstairs room.

While they were eating, Jesus said, "One of you will betray Me." The disciples were sad to hear this.

"Am I the one?" each asked.

"The one who dips his bread in the dish with Me is the one," Jesus answered. "I must die, but the man who betrays Me will be punished. It would be better if he had not been born."

Jesus took some bread and thanked God for it. Then He broke it and gave it to His friends.

"Take this and eat it," Jesus said. "This bread is My body."

Then Jesus took a cup and thanked God for it. He gave the cup to His friends. "This is My blood," He said. "It is poured out for many people to forgive their sins. I will not drink any more of this until I drink it with you in God's Kingdom."

When the supper was over, Jesus and His friends sang a hymn. Then they left for the Garden of Gethsemane.

Judas Betrays Jesus

Jesus was in the Garden of Gethsemane with His friends. He saw Judas coming with a mob. Judas knew Jesus would be here. He often came here with His friends, the disciples. Now Judas was bringing soldiers and guards from the religious leaders. They carried swords and clubs and torches.

Judas had given the mob a signal. The man I kiss is Jesus, he had told them.

Judas went to Jesus and said, "Teacher!"

"Do what you came to do," Jesus said to Judas. Judas kissed Jesus. Then some men came toward Jesus. "Who do you want?" Jesus asked.

"Jesus," they answered.

"I am Jesus," He said. The soldiers and guards fell to the ground. Then Jesus asked again, "Who do you want?"

"Jesus," they said.

"I told you I am Jesus," He said. "Why are you coming here for Me? I have taught each day in the temple. Now let these others go."

Peter had a sword. He struck Malchus, a servant of the high priest and cut off the man's right ear.

"Put that away," Jesus told Peter. "I could ask My Father and He would send twelve armies of angels. This must happen because the Bible said it would."

"Let these other men go," Jesus told the soldiers and guards. Then all of Jesus' disciples ran away. Someone grabbed Mark's cloak and pulled it off. He ran home naked.

Jesus Is Tried

When the soldiers and guards took Jesus to Jerusalem, they led Him to Annas. He had been the high priest. Now Caiaphas, his son-in-law, was the high priest.

Annas asked Jesus about His followers and His teachings. "I have taught in the open," Jesus said. "Ask the people who heard Me."

A guard slapped Jesus. "How dare You talk to the high priest like that!" he said.

Annas sent Jesus to Caiaphas. Jesus' hands were tied. The religious leaders were waiting there. They tried to find something wrong with Jesus. But they couldn't. Many told lies about Jesus. Two men said, "He claimed that He could build the temple in three days if it was torn down."

Jesus was quiet all the time. "Won't You answer?" Caiaphas demanded. "Tell me, are You the Messiah, God's Son?"

"I am," said Jesus. "Some day you will see Me at God's right hand, coming on the clouds of heaven."

Caiaphas tore his robe. "Blasphemy!" he shouted. "We don't need more witnesses. What do you say?"

"He must die," the other religious leaders said.

Some spit in Jesus' face. Some slapped Him. "Who hit You?" they mocked. "Tell us like a prophet."

Peter Denies Jesus

When the soldiers and guards took Jesus to Caiaphas' house, Peter went quietly into the courtyard. He stood with the guards, who warmed themselves by a charcoal fire.

Before long, a servant girl of the high priest stared at Peter. "You were with Jesus," she said.

"I don't know what you are talking about," Peter said. He left and went into a gateway. Then a rooster crowed.

While Peter was in the gateway another servant girl saw him. "He was with Jesus," she said. But Peter denied it.

About an hour later a man said, "You can't deny that you were with Jesus. You talk with a Galilean accent."

"I swear that I am telling the truth," Peter shouted. "I don't know what you are talking about." Peter began to curse. At that moment Jesus was led by. He stared at Peter. Then a rooster crowed again.

Suddenly Peter remembered what Jesus had said earlier. "Before the rooster crows twice, you will deny Me three times," Jesus had told him.

Peter ran out of the courtyard. He cried as if his heart was broken.

Jesus Is Crucified

"Nail Him to the cross," the Roman officer shouted. Roman soldiers nailed Jesus' hands and feet to the wooden cross. Then they set the cross up so people could watch Him die.

Near the cross, Roman soldiers threw some dice. They wanted Jesus' robe. It was like "drawing straws" to see who would get it. Jesus' mother and friends were there too. They were very sad to watch Jesus die. The sky grew very dark. The earth shook and groaned. Rocks burst in two. Dead people got up and walked around. God was showing people that Jesus was His Son.

The Romans ruled the land of Israel in Jesus' time. To them, crucifixion was much like the electric chair is today. It was their way of executing criminals.

But Jesus was not a criminal. The religious leaders had accused Him falsely. They hated Jesus. People were following Jesus instead of them. So they wanted to kill Jesus.

Jesus hung on the cross most of that day. Then He died. He died so that you and I could have our sins forgiven. This was God's plan from the very beginning. He planned for Jesus to die for you and me. He wants us to accept Jesus as our Savior. Then we can live with Him forever.

Jesus Rises from the Dead

Early on Sunday morning Jesus' mother Mary and some friends went to the tomb. That's where Jesus had been buried on Friday. They wanted to put some spices on His body. That's the way people did it at that time.

"Look," one of the women said. "The stone is rolled away from the tomb." They ran to see what had happened. But when they came to the tomb, they stopped and cried out. An angel stood near the doorway of the tomb.

"Don't be afraid," said the angel. "Jesus isn't here. He arose from the dead. He is alive. Look where He lay in the tomb."

Jesus certainly was not in the tomb now. So the women ran to tell the other disciples. This was Good News. It was the best news they had heard for a long time. Jesus had come back to life. He had risen!

Each Easter we sing wonderful songs about this morning long ago. We sing about Jesus, who arose from the dead. That shows us that He controls life and death. When He says, "You can live with Me forever," let's believe Him.

The Holy Spirit Comes at Pentecost

Seven weeks after Jesus died and arose from the dead, His followers met together. It was a special holiday called the Day of Pentecost.

Suddenly they heard a roaring sound, like a great wind blowing through the house where they met. Little flames of fire came upon each person's head. Then each person began speaking a foreign language. The Holy Spirit gave them the power to do this.

There were some people nearby who knew these languages. They were from the countries where the languages were spoken. They were amazed, for they knew Jesus' followers did not really know these foreign languages.

"How can this be?" they asked.

"These people are drunk!" some said.

But Peter gave a speech to the crowd.

"The Prophet Joel said this would happen. Many years ago he said that God would pour out His Spirit on the people," Peter said.

About 3,000 people believed what Peter said and were baptized that day. With Jesus' other followers they met to listen to the Apostles teach. They also met for prayer meetings and communion services.

Some of these believers sold what they owned and divided the money with other believers who needed it.

How thankful and happy Jesus' followers were as they met together in God's house, the temple, each day. They held small meetings together in other places, and they praised God for all that was happening. No wonder their neighbors seemed pleased with these people! Perhaps that is why more and more believers were added each day.

Peter and John Heal a Lame Man

It was time for the three o'clock worship service at the temple, God's house. Peter and John were going there to pray when they saw a crippled man beside the Beautiful Gate. This man came here every day to beg for money. Peter and John stopped to talk to him.

"Look at me!" said Peter. The man looked, expecting some money.

"We have no money to give you," said Peter. "But we have another gift. In the name of Jesus, get up and walk!"

Peter took the man by the hand and lifted him to his feet. Suddenly the man's feet were healed and he began to leap and walk. Then he began to jump around, praising God. He even ran into God's house.

You can imagine how surprised people were to see the crippled beggar jumping around. But Peter said, "Why are you so surprised? We didn't do this. God did this so He could honor Jesus. This is the same Jesus that you killed in ignorance. But we have seen Him alive. Now He wants you to turn away from your sins."

Stephen Is Stoned

Stephen was filled with faith and the power of the Holy Spirit. He did amazing miracles among the people. Of course there were some people who did not like this preaching and miracle-working.

One day, some members of "The Freedmen," a Jewish cult, began to argue with Stephen. Some other Jewish men joined in. Stephen was so wise and had such a wonderful way about him that no one could find anything wrong with him. So these men found some wicked fellows to lie about Stephen. They said he had cursed Moses and God.

These lying men stirred up the crowds against Stephen so the Jewish leaders arrested him and had him taken to the Council. This was the court where the leaders decided what to do with people like Stephen.

The lying men told the Council that Stephen was saying terrible things about the temple, God's house, and about God's laws. When the members of the Council looked at Stephen, they saw that his face glowed like an angel's face.

"Are these things true?" the High Priest asked Stephen.

Stephen gave a long speech to the Council. "Your ancestors killed the prophets, and you killed God's Son," he told them. These leaders were furious. The leaders and their people dragged Stephen out of the city of Jerusalem. Then they took off their cloaks and laid them at the feet of a young man named Saul. Later he would become the Apostle Paul, but now he was one of those killing Stephen. Then these people threw big stones at Stephen until he died.

"Lord let me go to be with You," Stephen prayed. "And please don't punish these men for their sin." When Stephen said that, he died.

Saul Is Converted

Saul was getting worse now in his persecution of the believers. One day he went to the High Priest and asked to go to the synagogues of Damascus. Saul wanted to find believers there and put them in prison. But when he came near Damascus, a bright light suddenly flashed from the sky. Saul fell to the ground.

"Saul, why are you hurting Me like this?" a voice from heaven asked.

"Who are you, Lord?" Saul asked.

"I am Jesus. You are hurting Me," the voice said. "Get up and go into Damascus. You will be told what to do."

When Saul got up, he realized he was blind. So his companions led him to Damascus, where he remained blind for three days.

Meanwhile, in Damascus, a believer named Ananias had a vision. "Go to the house of Judas on Straight Street and ask for Saul of Tarsus," God told Ananias. "He is waiting for you."

Ananias was afraid. "But he is a terrible man," Ananias argued.

"Do what I tell you," God said. "I have chosen Saul to be a special missionary. He must suffer many things for Me."

Ananias went and found Saul. He put his hands on him and said, "Jesus has sent me to do this so you will be filled with the Holy Spirit and can see again." Just as if scales fell from his eyes, Saul could see again. Then he was baptized.

After Saul ate he got his strength again. Saul stayed there with the believers of Damascus a few days. He went to the synagogue at Damascus to tell them that Jesus is God's Son. The people at the synagogue were quite surprised to hear Saul preach like this. "Isn't this the man who hurt so many believers in Jerusalem?" they asked.

Saul Escapes in a Basket

Saul had hated the people who believed in Jesus. He had hurt many of them. He even came to Damascus to hurt Jesus' followers there. But on the way, Jesus spoke to him from heaven. Saul accepted Jesus as his Savior, too.

Now Saul was preaching about Jesus. He even went into the synagogues and preached to his old friends. Of course this surprised them. Before long, they grew angry and planned to kill Saul. But Saul heard about this plot.

Each day and each night these men watched the gates of Damascus to catch Saul when he went out. They would kill him. But Saul's new friends, those who believed in Jesus, put Saul in a basket one night. Then they let him down through an opening in the wall.

Saul escaped to Jerusalem, but Jesus' followers were afraid to accept him. Then Barnabas told the Apostles how Saul had accepted Jesus and how he had preached with much courage in Damascus. Now the believers accepted Saul and he worked with them in Jerusalem.

Before long, some enemies tried to kill Saul, so the believers took him to the seaport at Caesarea, and sent him to his hometown of Tarsus.

Peter Raises Dorcas from the Dead

Tabitha was a wonderful Christian woman who was always helping the poor. Some people called her Dorcas, which meant gazelle. Perhaps that was because she was always running around doing special things for people. Dorcas lived in Joppa, just a few miles northwest of Lydda, where Peter had healed Aeneas.

After she died, her friends washed her body and laid it in an upstairs room. Then they sent two men to Peter. "Come quickly," they urged.

When Peter came to the house, Dorcas' friends took him upstairs to the place where they had put her body. Widows gathered around Peter, crying as they showed him all the cloaks and other clothing Dorcas had made for them. Peter asked everyone to leave the room. Then he knelt and prayed.

"Get up!" he said to Dorcas. Suddenly she opened her eyes, looked at Peter, and sat up. Peter took her by the hand and lifted her up. Then he called the widows and other believers in and presented her to them alive.

Before long, the news of this miracle spread all over Joppa. Many believed in Jesus because of this.

Peter Is Put into Prison and Escapes

King Herod began to arrest the Christians and persecute them. He executed John's brother, James, with a sword. He put Peter in prison and put a guard of four squads of four soldiers each to watch him. After the Passover, he would put Peter on trial.

The Christians began to pray earnestly while Peter was in prison. The night before Peter would go on trial, he was sleeping between two soldiers, bound by chains. Soldiers guarded the entrance. Suddenly an angel of the Lord appeared and a light shone in the prison cell. The angel struck Peter's side to wake him.

"Get up!" the angel said. Then the chains fell from Peter's wrists. "Put on your clothes and sandals," the angel said. "Follow me."

Peter did what the angel said and followed him from the prison. The iron gate opened and they walked down the street. Then the angel disappeared.

Peter headed for the house of Mary, John Mark's mother. Christians were praying there for Peter. Peter knocked on the courtyard door and a servant girl named Rhoda answered. She knew it was Peter's voice and was so happy that she ran to tell the others. Rhoda was so excited she forgot to open the door.

"Peter is at the door!" she cried out.

"You're crazy," the others said. "It must be his angel." But she insisted that he was there and Peter kept on knocking. At last they let him in. Then Peter had them be quiet. After he told them what had happened, he left.

There was quite a stir the next day at the prison. Herod executed the guards, then went to Caesarea where he put on royal robes and gave a speech.

"This is a god!" some people shouted. Herod accepted their praise, but God was angry and struck him down with worms so that he died.

Paul Begins His Travels for Jesus

"I have a special work for Barnabas and Paul," the Holy Spirit said. The Christians at Antioch prayed and put their hands on these two men. Then they sent them on a trip. These men would tell people in other countries about Jesus. John Mark went with them.

The first stop was Cyprus. The governor, Sergius Paulus, invited the men to tell him about Jesus. But a magician named Bar-Jesus tried to keep the governor from believing.

"You are working against God," Paul told him. "God will make you blind for a while." Suddenly Bar-Jesus was blind, begging for someone to lead him.

The next stop was Perga. For some reason John Mark, who later wrote the Gospel of Mark, left Paul and Barnabas and went home to Jerusalem.

Paul and Barnabas went on to Antioch in Pisidia. On the Sabbath they went to the synagogue. Paul preached a sermon about Jesus. "He is the Messiah, God's Son," Paul said.

"Come back next week," the people said. "We want to hear more."

Paul and Barnabas came back the next Sabbath. Almost everyone in town came too. But the synagogue leaders were jealous when they saw the big crowd. They argued with Paul and insulted him.

"We had to bring the Good News to you first," Paul told them. "But you have rejected it. Now we will take it to the Gentiles." The Gentiles were glad to hear this. Many of them believed. Then the synagogue leaders stirred up trouble and made Paul and Barnabas leave town.

The Prison at Philippi

Paul and his friends stayed several days at Philippi. One day as they were going to pray a slave girl met them. She had an evil spirit in her. The girl's owners made much money because this girl was a fortune-teller.

"In Jesus' name, I command you to come out of that girl!" Paul shouted. The evil spirit came out at that moment.

The girl's owners were angry. They knew they could not make money from the girl now. So they grabbed Paul and Silas and dragged them to the town officials in the public square. "These Jews are causing trouble here," they said. "They are teaching things against our law. We cannot let them do this." Soon the crowd that had gathered was against Paul and Silas.

The officials tore the clothes from Paul and Silas. They had them beaten and thrown into the inner prison with large blocks of wood fastened to their feet.

About midnight Paul and Silas were praying and singing. The other prisoners listened. Suddenly an earthquake shook the prison. The doors opened and the chains fell from the prisoners. When the jailer saw this he tried to kill himself. He would be tortured if he let these men escape.

"Don't hurt yourself." Paul said. "We are all here."

Then the jailer rushed in with a light, he fell down before Paul and Silas. He was trembling. "What must I do to be saved?" he asked.

"Believe in the Lord Jesus," Paul answered. "Then you and your family will be saved." Paul then told the jailer and the others in his house about Jesus.

The jailer washed Paul's wounds. Then he and his family were baptized. The jailer and his family were happy now because they were Christians.

Paul at Mars Hill

Paul was waiting in Athens for Silas and Timothy. As he looked around the city he became upset at the many idols he saw.

At the synagogue, Paul talked to Jews and Greeks who worshiped God. He also went to the marketplace each day to talk with the people there.

Some Epicurean and Stoic teachers argued with Paul. But he told them the Good News, how Jesus rose from the dead.

"He's dreaming," they said. "He doesn't know what he is saying. He must be teaching about some foreign religion."

These men took Paul to Mars Hill. It was also called Areopagus. The city council was there. These men wanted to hear what Paul was saying. "We want to know what these things mean," they said. People in Athens spent most of their time talking about new things.

Paul spoke to the city council. "You people of Athens are very religious," he said. "You even have an altar to an unknown god." Then Paul talked about God and His Son Jesus.

When the people of Athens heard Paul talk about rising from the dead some made fun of him. Others asked to hear him again. One council member became a Christian, along with a woman named Damaris, and some others.

Paul Is Arrested

When Paul went back to Jerusalem, he visited the temple. But some people of Asia who hated him saw him there. They began to shout. "Help! This man is doing bad things here in our holy temple," they shouted.

A mob rushed at Paul and dragged him out of the temple. Then the temple doors were closed. The mob began to beat Paul. They wanted to kill him, but some Roman soldiers came and took him away.

The Roman commander put Paul in chains. "Who is he and what has he done?" he asked. But he got many answers. "Kill him," the mob kept shouting. The next day the commander took Paul to the council of religious leaders. He wanted to find why Paul was in trouble. But when Paul said he was a Pharisee, the Pharisees were for him and the Sadducees were against him.

The following day more than 40 men plotted together. They would not eat or drink until they had killed Paul. Paul's nephew, the son of Paul's sister, heard about this and told the army commander.

By nine that night the commander left Jerusalem with 200 soldiers and 70 horsemen and 200 spearmen. They took Paul with them on a horse.

Commander Claudius Lysias sent a letter with Paul and the soldiers. It told Governor Felix at Caesarea why Paul was sent to him.

That night the group camped at Antipatris. The foot soldiers came back to Jerusalem the next day and the others took Paul to Caesarea. They turned Paul over to Governor Felix and went home.

"I will hear you when your accusers come," the governor said. Then he put Paul with guards in the palace built by Herod.

Paul Before Governors and Kings

Paul was in prison in the palace at Caesarea. Five days after he came there Ananias came with other religious leaders. Ananias had been the high priest before his son-in-law Caiaphas.

These men brought a lawyer named Tertullus. He said that Paul was a trouble-maker. He said that Paul was trying to hurt the temple.

Governor Felix let Paul speak next. Paul said he had done nothing wrong. If he did, what was it?

Felix kept Paul guarded after the trial. But he let him have more freedom. He even asked Paul to tell him about Jesus from time to time. After two long years passed Porcius Festus became governor in place of Felix.

Festus had another trial. Again the religious leaders from Jerusalem came. Again they spoke lies about Paul. "Will you go to Jerusalem to be tried?" Festus asked.

"No, I want Caesar to judge me," Paul answered. He knew he would not get a fair trial in Jerusalem with those men.

Since Paul was a Roman citizen, he could ask for Caesar to judge him. So Festus agreed to let him go to Rome to see Caesar.

A few days later King Agrippa and Bernice came to Caesarea. Agrippa wanted to hear Paul. So Paul was brought before him. When Agrippa heard Paul he said, "He has done nothing wrong. He could be set free if he had not asked to go to Caesar."

Plans were made to send Paul to Rome. There he would be tried by the Roman Emperor, who was called Caesar.

Paul Sails and Is Shipwrecked

Paul had asked for Caesar, the Roman Emperor, to judge him. He knew he would not get a fair trial in Jerusalem. The religious leaders there hated him. So plans were made to send Paul to Rome.

Julius, an officer in the emperor's army, guarded Paul and some other prisoners. Julius was kind to Paul. When the ship came to Sidon, he let Paul visit friends. They gave Paul what he needed for his trip.

But sailing was hard. The wind was blowing toward the ship. It took much longer than they thought. By the time the ship reached Safe Harbors, on the island of Crete, it was getting too late to sail. The sea would soon be dangerous.

One day a strong "Northeaster" wind blew. It blew them far off course. For 14 days the storm kept up. All 276 men on the ship thought they would die.

One night the ship came near land. The sailors put out four anchors. They threw all the grain from the ship into the sea. Then they waited for morning.

When morning came the sailors saw land. They cut the ropes to the anchors. They sailed for the land. But the ship hit a sandbar and broke into pieces. Some men swam to shore. Others went on boards.

It was raining and cold when the men came to land, an island called Melita. Today it is called Malta. The people built a fire to warm these men.

Suddenly a poisonous snake came from some sticks and bit Paul. When he did not die the people thought he was a god. The shipwrecked people stayed three months on this island. An important man named Publius took care of them. Paul healed Publius' father. He also healed others on the island. So the people were kind to Paul and the other men. They gave them all they needed.

Paul at Rome

A ship from Alexandria had stayed at Melita for the winter. When it was time to go, this ship took Paul and the others toward Rome. They landed at a port called Puteoli. From there Paul would be taken to Rome on one of the Roman roads.

Some Christians came to meet Paul. They asked Paul to stay with them for a week. Then they went on toward Rome. When they were about 40 miles from Rome, some Christians from Rome came to meet them. This was a place called the Forum on the Appian Way. Others joined them at a place called the Three Inns. Paul thanked God for these Christians. He felt much better when he saw them.

In Rome, Paul was allowed to live in a rented house. He had a Roman guard with him at all times. Many people came to see him. He told them all about Jesus.

Three days after Paul arrived, he invited the Jewish leaders in Rome to meet with him. He told them about Jesus and showed them how the Old Testament was about Him. Some of them became Christians. Others would not believe.

For two years, Paul lived in Rome, waiting for his trial. While he was there, he told many people the Good News about Jesus. He had great courage and did not worry about getting into trouble. And no one kept him from teaching and preaching about Jesus.